THE BOOK OF THE DEAD.

THE BOOK OF THE DEAD.

BY

GEORGE H. BOKER.

TU MIHI SOLUS ERAS.

PHILADELPHIA:
J. B. LIPPINCOTT & CO.
LONDON: 16 SOUTHAMPTON STREET, STRAND.
1882.

Beside the spreading Nile of old,
They buried with their worthy dead
A scrolled papyrus, to unfold
His virtues and the life he led.

And all the gods, in council grave,
Asked nothing but this written scroll,
As evidence, to doom or save
The bearer's arbitrated soul.

Grand thought! enlarging on the view;
This winnowed record of the pen
Made truth a right, and upward drew
The moral sympathies of men.

Man leaned on man for judgment just,
  The grave became truth's inner shrine,
And every heap of mortal dust
  Was reverenced as a thing divine.

So I within thy hallowed tomb
  Enclose this book, most loved of men!
There, till the dreadful day of doom,
  May it repose, but open then!

Book of the Dead, if any see
  False judgments in thy earnest page,
Be all thy gathered sins on me,—
  Man's vengeance and God's juster rage!

I.

'Tis not my purpose to explain
  The truths here dimly set in view;
These hieroglyphics of the brain
  Are meant for others to undo.

I hang my painted pictures high,
  I paint them ill, or paint them well;
If they say nothing to the eye,
  Then I have nothing more to tell.

Thus much, howe'er, to all be known:
  The man, of men most loved by me,
Raised up a ruin till it shone
  Before men's eyes a prodigy.

And all men praised the wondrous spot,
  And marvelled daily more and more;
The only fault was he forgot
  To drive the vermin from the door.

The knaves who found safe shelter there,
  Who owed him more than they could pay,
Were eaten up with envious care
  Because their chief was more than they.

But, cowards shrewd, they hid their thought,
  And fetched and carried at his nod,
Until his soul was upward caught
  By the dread, sudden hand of God.

In life they played their cunning parts,
  They lauded everything he did;
In death they—bold, heroic hearts—
  Stabbed at him through the coffin-lid!

They searched his mansion through and through,
  With wolfish hate in every glance;
Of all they saw they nothing knew,
  And charged him with their ignorance.

Here was some work left incomplete,
  There something showed the touch of time;
They could not fill his empty seat,—
  They made his very death a crime.

Then slander followed, hints of guilt,
  The murmur grew a general roar;
And, in the very house he built,
  They drove his children from the door.

Now partly in my scorn of wrong,
  But chiefly for the wronged one's love,
I lift my voice, and through my song
  I hear an answer from above.

If you who judge, charge any leaf
  With thoughts too wild or words too plain,
Then say, the man is mad with grief;
  These villains struck through heart and brain.

II.

This cross between a curse and psalm
  I utter with a holy scorn,
I lift my pierced and bleeding palm,
  I point you where the nail has torn.

I drag to light a private grief,
  I brandish it before your eyes;
Not that the action gives relief,
  Nor asks to hear another's sighs.

I checked awhile the brimming tide,
  I held it backward from the world;
It burst at last, and far and wide
  Flames ran, and burning stones were hurled.

This grief of mine my soul had stirred
  To song, had never poet sung;
There are some wrongs that will be heard,
  That find or make themselves a tongue.

I move by some mysterious law,
  The law that makes the singer sing,
Though the sharp draught these miscreants draw
  Be, to their class, a wholesome thing.

The tears that mingle with the bane
  Are holy, and in mercy given;
Let no man wipe away their stain;
  I wish to show the marks in heaven.

It humbles me that I must use,
  At times, the shape of common woes;
But mourners' robes are few to choose;
  Like utterance from like sorrow flows.

Outstretched I hold my acrid cup,
  I ask no grace from king or clown;
The hardy hand that takes it up,
  May curse me when he sets it down.

III.

Let him who dares usurp God's right
  To sit in judgment on the dead,
Be sure no trace of sinful blight
  Corrupts his heart or wrongs his head.

Let him be sure that all is fair
  Within his round of sin-born clay;
That penance long and fast and prayer
  Have purged his grosser parts away.

He should be guilt and passion free
  To whom this awful cause is given,
And like Elijah stand, when he
  Stepped in the flesh from earth to heaven.

With humble soul, and reverence deep,
  He should approach the holy gloom;
And lowly kneel, and lowly weep:
  Not, like a vandal, burst the tomb.

And when the coffin-lid is raised,
  Where lies the dumb, defenceless man,
Let him remember those who praised,
  And count his virtues if he can.

We judge the act and consequence,
  We blindly hit the truth perchance;
But God looks through this film of sense;
  He weighs the heart and circumstance.

What in our eyes is glaring crime,
  In God's may be a thing to bless;
Our eyes see ill through space and time;
  We cannot know, we can but guess.

Let him who judges have a fear
  Lest hearts be wrung and eyes made dim,
And tremble lest an orphan's tear
  May curse his sacrilege and him.

And when the final verdict 's made,
  Stretch not the law to meet the case;
Stern Justice lays aside her blade
  When gazing in a dead man's face.

Keeping this solemn charge at heart,
  Draw near the grave, and lay it bare;
Assume your self-appointed part;—
  Now judge the dead man, if you dare!

IV.

I MAKE a pageant of my pain,
  Some say, throughout my dreary song,
And mar the sweetness of my strain
  With dismal groans at crime and wrong.

It may be so: I can but sing;
  For thus one half my grief is drowned:
The wild bird, struck beneath the wing,
  Recks little how his note may sound.

This cry of pain invades the land,
  It fills my ears, it will not pass;
Life's brightest and most golden sand
  Runs grating through the narrow glass.

I do not say our journey goes
  Without some roses, there and here;
Although short seasons has the rose,
  The thorns are growing all the year.

I quarrel not with human mirth;
  I envy not the man who steals
His hard-wrung pleasures from the earth,
  And swings the wine-cup till he reels.

I shall not enter at his door
  With doleful songs, to move his scorn;
May roses crown him o'er and o'er!
  I sing for him who feels the thorn.

I care not who are deaf, who hear:
  Amidst the people's groan and shout,
I sing as nature wills; the ear
  'Twould hear my song must seek it out.

And if it be a moan or sigh,
  Unwelcome, foolish, as you deem,
I pray you pass me lightly by,
  And leave the dreamer to his dream.

V.

To-day my inmost soul was stirred:
I saw the crocus from the ground
Burst, like a little flame, and heard
The wandering bluebird's trumpet sound.

The heat of life is in the air,
And recreated Summer swings
Her first faint odors here and there,
To lure the bee's adventurous wings.

What if my soul should strain the chain
That binds her to this silent grave,
And long o'er hill and vale again
The pinion of her youth to wave?

Go forth, O soul, and take thy flight!
Dash through the meadows' fiery bloom!
I know thou wilt return ere night,
And sink and settle in the tomb.

VI.

THY grave is shut against the lies
  Of this false world. Thou art at rest,
With eyelids pressed on sightless eyes,
  Palms crossed above thy breathless breast.

The fretful stir of sense is gone;
  Thou canst not hear these miscreants roar.
I, passion-fraught, I hear alone —
  Alone, and thank my God therefore!

Or if from heaven's far crystal height
  Thy disembodied soul can see,
Earth's gayest or most solemn sight
  May seem a phantasm to thee.

Our comic and our tragic play
  To thee are but illusions vain,
Theatric shows that pass away
  In smiles, or leave a pleasing pain.

Majestic Soul, rebuke me not,
If, while I fill this narrow stage,
My higher nature is forgot,
Lost in the actor's painted rage.

To me this scene is all in all;
I am the thing I seem to be:
The bell will ring, the curtain fall,
I pass into reality.

VII.

If this cruel cup of love and hate
  Shall pass to other lips than mine,
And mortals, of an older date,
  Make mouths above my bitter wine;

And cry, "Behold, he gives our thirst
  A sponge of vinegar and gall!"
I answer, Bear my cross accurst,
  And this fell draught shall not appall.

Nay, rather merciful and mild,
  To such a thirst, the draught will seem;
For one with raging famine wild
  Drinks gladly at the foulest stream.

O solemn line, arrayed in black,
  That shades you to the inmost heart,
Who tread the wide funereal track
  On which earth's fated mourners start!—

The long procession, never done,
  That wearies out the countless years,
Whose march is timed by sob and groan,
  And watered with perpetual tears;—

I know you by your shuddering sighs,
  Your lips severe, your figures bent,
And thus, beneath your downcast eyes,
  I spread my awful sacrament!

VIII.

Sometimes I weary of my task,
And cease to ply my vengeful thong;
And of my judgment coldly ask,
Are these dull cattle worth a song?

Shall I preserve in studied rhyme
Each ignominious villain's name,
And give him, in the after-time,
An immortality of shame?

Shall they, hung on the sweeping skirts
Of coming years, drag out their doom,
While men of shy but pure deserts
Are mouldering in a nameless tomb?

I half repent my own device:
Like ancient Egypt's erring priests,
I waste my precious oil and spice,
Embalming coarse and vulgar beasts.

Sure even in these slow, drudging days,
  Are men whose hearts and deeds are bright,
Who well deserve a poet's lays:
  Thus struck, I turn to heaven for light.

But as to God's eternal blue,
  I lift my love-devoted head,
From inner depths come gliding through
  The stern, cold features of the dead.

I bow, I weep; I cannot choose;
  In vain imploring pity cries;
In vain I falter or refuse
  Beneath the mandate of those eyes.

Once more the scourge in fury beats,
  The writhing culprits feel their fate,
And love, unconquerable, completes
  The intermitted task of hate.

IX.

I HEAR the clarions of the day,
Night's misty veil is upward drawn,
And with its golden fringes play
The jewelled fingers of the dawn.

The curling vapors, one by one,
Are shot with opalescent gleams,
And, now, the almost risen sun
Darts up a thousand crimson streams.

From heaven to earth the splendor steals,
Down gilded vanes to windowed towers;
The conscious bells break out in peals,—
God! what a wondrous world is ours!

The fiery colors slowly fade,
In sapphire depths they pass away;
The sun begins his grand parade,
From pole to pole 'tis perfect day.

Earth's children feel their mother warm,
  From drowsy beds they wake and start,
And forth, through streets and alleys, swarm
  In myriads to the noisy mart.

Oh! happy toil! Oh! blessed fate!
  To no one thought too close confined,
That, with each motion, drops a date,
  And shifts the pictures of the mind.

I envy you your changing strife,
  Your weary hours, your evening rest,
When all the little cares of life
  Are lulled to slumber in the breast:

For my poor soul, that still will float
  Near one idea of stern device,
Drifts on, like the Laplander's boat,
  Close moored beside its berg of ice.

X.

If passion less, and reason more,
My wayward nature checked and led,
If some great change of empire bore
The seat of rule from heart to head;

If, with the dullards, I inclined
To count my gold, and drop to clay,
And leave the fingered stuff behind,
To witness me to such as they;

If I could trim my muse's wing,
Control her flight, abate her rage,
And teach her, a well-ordered thing,
To coo and warble in a cage;

If I could school my face to show
A visored hate, a vapid love,
And range my feelings in a row,
For any fool at will to move;

If I could lie and feign, to draw
  My simple neighbor in a trap,
Just on the outskirts of the law,
  Securely sheltered from mishap;

If that, to which all hearts are sold,
  Could be the god on which I call,—
That greasy harlot, common gold,
  The temptress of man's second fall;

If in my soul the Lord were dead,
  And conscience dumb and pitiless,
And Aaron's golden calf instead
  Stared o'er the moral wilderness;

Why, then, this servile world would praise
  The very ground on which I stood,
And the base scoundrels of these lays
  Would hail me of their brotherhood.

XI.

PETER and Judas merged in one!
Two traitors, matchless till thy time,
It needs to show the deed thou hast done,
And fill the measure of thy crime.

Him thou deniedst, and sold to men,
Was more to thee than aught on earth;
He raised thy narrow fortunes when
The world was cold before thy worth.

Change places with that noble heart;
If thou wert dead and wronged, would he,
I ask thee, act so vile a part
In dealing with thy memory?

Oh, fie! conceal thy dirty gold,
Thy secret comfort, open shame!
For thirty pieces thou hast sold
The treasure of an honest name.

Or else let Judas' story yield
  Its fullest fruit: Take up thy pelf,
Seek out the Potter, buy his field,
  And in some corner hang thyself!

XII.

WHILE this shall stand, the wicked deeds
  Of these base men shall never die:
A thousand years the wheaten seeds
  Within the mummy's palms may lie;—

A thousand years, and once again
  A light breaks in upon the tomb,
And from those dusty hands the grain
  Is sown, o'er harvest-fields to bloom.

And so may sleep my angry rhymes,
  And you may say, "The fellow raves!"
I smile: these lines, in after-times,
  Shall drag you naked from your graves.

And save the record I have made,
  Your lives shall have no history,
And that shall cast a baleful shade
  Upon your shameful progeny.

XIII.

THE regicides who slew King Charles,
  And won the realm, and bore the sway,
Were, like yourselves, but vulgar carls,
  Yet, like yourselves, they had their day.

For years they held the kingdom fast,
  And all their future days looked fair;
And when from earth they grandly passed,
  They left it to their children's care.

But time set all their wrongs to rights;
  When prone lay every Roundhead cur,
Their fathers' skulls were ghastly sights,
  All grinning over Westminster.

XIV.

I HAD a vision of the night,
  A presage of the day of doom,
When all the wrongs shall come to light
  That slumber in the darkened tomb.

I saw the court of heaven unclose,
  The risen sinners sadly meet;
Our good, our ill, our joys, our woes,
  Stood naked at the judgment-seat.

My culprits found a foremost place.
  I gazed on them: I bore no grudge
Before his stern, accusing face,
  I witness, and our God the judge.

I gazed on them, I gazed around;
  No passion held me in control;
The sense of awe was so profound,
  So deep the clearness of the soul!

The knave by whom the band was led,
  His scarlet face was pallid grown,
The crimson hair upon his head
  Rose up, as if it were his own.

Some showed a guilty, downcast look,
  And some their aching vision screened
From the terrific light that shook
  These twelve apostles of the fiend.

And he who had betrayed the dead,
  When those cold eyes upon him fell,
To shun that glance, ere aught was said,
  Slunk downward into endless hell.

The cause was judged, the verdict given,
  So plain that every soul might hear;
And the great truth was blown through heaven,
  From golden clarions, far and near.

Now let men judge, as men think right,
  They only see as men may see:
I had a vision of the night,
  By gracious God 'twas sent to me.

XV.

THE moon sails up the mottled sky,
  Half hidden in a fleecy shroud,
And from the east, with sword on high,
  Orion plunges through the cloud.

The west is clear. One solemn star
  Looks at its image in the wave:
The star seems very sad and far;
  It bends above my loved one's grave.

Was that a rushing of the wind,
  A noise of beasts, a shriek for aid,
Or cry of vampires, fury-blind,
  That hunger where my dead is laid?

Forth through the moonlight, towards the glow
  Of yon lone star, I take my way;
And at thy hillock bending low,
  I sing to thee a tender lay.

The vampires' howl was fierce and high;
  It sinks to silence, and they flit
Back to their noisome dens, while I
  Make a faint music where I sit.

XVI.

When the dead Cid was laid in state,
  His body armed, his trophies near,
A caitiff Jew, inflamed with hate,
  Stole through the chancel to the bier.

Amid the candle-light he stood,
  And peered into the warrior's face,
To curse, in his vindictive mood,
  That stern despiser of his race.

His fury kindled as he cursed,
  He scorned the dead, he grinned, he jeered;
His courage rose, he did his worst,
  He plucked the hero by the beard.

The pale face flushed, and instant rang
  A clamor through the startled night;
With sword half drawn, the corpse upsprang;
  The Hebrew fled in mad affright.

If thou, poor corpse, that 'mid this band
  Of slanderous churls so still dost lie,
Couldst move one finger of thy hand,
  How would these Jews in terror fly!

XVII.

If yon cold lizard, sliming o'er
  The sacred tablet of the dead,
Had been half human at the core,
  These bitter tears had ne'er been shed.

Had he possessed a common soul,
  A faith in God, a heart, a brain,
I ne'er had penned this dreadful scroll,
  And my bruised heart might heal again.

Had he but shown a decent sense
  Of what is due the giver's hand,
But paid for gold with copper pence,
  This shame had vanished from the land.

I little hoped from thee; in fact,
  I knew how thin thy cold blood ran;
I only thought to see thee act,
  Not as a hero, as a man.

XVIII.

FALSE Pilate washed his guilty hands
  Before the congregated Jews,
And said, "Behold, this just man stands
  Acquitted; why is he accused?"

But when they cried more eagerly,
  Appalled the trembling coward stood;
And said, "Bear witness, I am free!
  Upon you be his guiltless blood!"

'Twas Pilate's part to bind or loose;
  To yield his functions, at the stir
Of threatening tongues, was vain excuse,
  And Pilate was a murderer.

XIX.

OFT when thy duties bound thee down
 To wearying labor, I, more free,
Fled from the stagnant heat of town,
 And sought to lure thee after me.

In vain I tried the oriole's call,
 In vain the robin's tender note,
In vain the woodland songsters all
 Made music in my swelling throat.

In vain I shook the morning spray
 From blossom-boughs, or round thee blew
The odor of the new-mown hay
 From hill-sides steaming with the dew.

Or painted nature's sterner moods,—
 The flashing cloud, the driving rain,
When through the slant and groaning woods
 Roars the terrific hurricane.

Or to the mountains bare and bleak,
  Through gulfs, through crags, o'er ledges clomb,
And showed how from the cloven peak
  The streams plunge out in clouds of foam.

Or lightly touched on pastoral joys,—
  The woolly flock, the grazing kine;
What simple things are Damon's toys,
  How Chloe's milky buckets shine!

Or with the ocean's moaning cry,
  Bewailed thy absence from afar;
Or mounting to the darkening sky,
  Gazed at thee from the evening star.

In vain I pled with all my art;
  I had no power to move thee then;
Thy joys were in the human heart,
  Amidst the press and throng of men.

I pointed to the o'erworked dust
  That swells the church-yard mounds: you said,
"'Twere better to wear out than rust:
  There is rest enough amongst the dead."

Poor soul, I mourn thy labor lost;
  Thy self-denying purpose gained,
But gained at a prodigious cost,—
  Thy work denied, thy memory stained.

I may misjudge. Thy life to thee,
  Perhaps, was filled with joyous hours,
And seemed as fair an empery
  As that o'er which the poet towers.

'Tis for omniscient God alone
  To know who grovels, who ascends:
We work His purpose, one by one,
  In divers ways, to divers ends.

XX.

THE chain that binds me to this oar
  Is galling to my sentient soul;
My spirits, fretted sick and sore,
  In endless anguish toss and roll.

The face of heaven is hard and black,
  Gaunt nature scorns my human woe,
The tardy arm of God is slack,
  And hell a far-off, painted show.

God's ear is deaf to wrong or right;
  In vain my ceaseless prayer I pour,
Through painful day and troubled night,
  For simple justice, nothing more.

They bask and fatten in the sun,
  These schemers, and they grin with mirth
At every cunning wrong they have done
  To truth, to right, to buried worth.

I read of grand old Hebrew days,
  When God judged earth, and I but see,
In all that scribe or prophet says,
  The wreck of dead mythology.

This world of ours, this modern world,
  That seeks no heaven, and shuns no hell,
By art and science forward hurled,
  Gets on without a God as well.

So sick at heart, in angry mood,
  I throw my bitter pen aside,
And cry, "Why care for ill or good,
  Or any end that may betide?

"I'll live my life, I'll branch and bloom,
  I'll kill the conscience in my breast:
So from this dreadful work of doom
  My hand shall have eternal rest!"

I hear the swift descending rush
  Of angel wings, the hovering play,
The rustle, and the awful hush
  That follows, as they fold away.

I know who stands beside my chair,
  Who sternly motions to my pen;
I grasp it, in foredoomed despair,
  And ply my fearful task again.

Once more the pinions are unfurled,
  They beat the air, they mount on high,
And from this low, sin-bounded world,
  Go fanning gently up the sky.

XXI.

For gold you did your treacherous deed,
Mere money was your aim and end;
To selfish lust you gave good heed,
And turned against your helpless friend.

The only chance fate e'er bestowed,
Where power was given you to repay,
In scanty weight, the debt you owed,
Your craft used only to betray.

The vilest baseness of your kind—
The miser's greed, the coward's fear—
I grant your nature, yet I find
Nowhere in human kind your peer.

Since the world's history began,
No record stands of one who sold
So broadly, in the face of man,
His buried friend for dirty gold.

Poor Judas, for his thirty pence,
  A living victim dared to sell;
And when he saw the consequence,
  Fell riven with the pangs of hell.

But to the treachery of the Jew
  You join the dastard, and instead
Of bartering with your sordid crew
  For one alive, you sell the dead.

Is gold to conscience bolt and bar,
  Against all entrance sound and firm?
I fear it cannot heal the scar
  Gnawed through by the undying worm.

No man will envy you your prize;
  I hold the treasure dearly bought;
I only see before your eyes
  A bag of gold, a hell of thought.

XXII.

I STAND beside the sea once more,
Its measured murmur comes to me;
The breeze is low upon the shore,
And low upon the purple sea.

Across the bay the flat sand sweeps,
To where the helméd light-house stands
Upon its post, and vigil keeps,
Far seaward marshalling all the lands.

The hollow surges rise and fall,
The ships steal up the quiet bay;
I scarcely hear or see at all,
My thoughts are flown so far away.

They follow on yon sea-bird's track,
Beyond the beacon's crystal dome;
They will not falter, nor come back,
Until they find my darkened home.

Ah! woe is me! 'tis scarce a year
  Since, gazing o'er this moaning main,
My thoughts flew home without a fear,
  And with content returned again.

To-day, alas! the fancies dark,
  That from my laden bosom flew,
Returning, came into the ark,
  Not with the olive, with the yew.

The ships draw slowly towards the strand,
  The watchers' hearts with hope beat high;—
But ne'er again wilt thou touch land,
  Lost, lost in yonder sapphire sky!

XXIII.

THE noblest heart I ever knew
  Died when thine ceased to rise and fall:
My loves, indeed, are shy and few;
  My love for thee was crown of all.

I loved thee for thy honest scorn
  Of fraud and wrong, thy tender ruth,
That touched the lowest thing forlorn,
  Thy eagle grasp on right and truth.

I never knew thy tongue to hang,
  Before rich wrong, in selfish fright;
But I have heard it when it rang,
  A clarion, on the side of right.

The clearness of thy mental view
  Embraced all objects that it sought,
And pierced the darkest avenue
  Of high and speculative thought.

It wisely taught the proud and rich,
  It roused the poor man's humble fire,
And sometimes even struck the pitch,
  To tune my false and jarring lyre.

Where'er it fell, a ray was shed,
  Some truth revealed, some reason found;
Like a revolving light, it spread
  The whole horizon round and round.

We children laud the hero's prize,
  The outward Christian's patent worth;
Forgetting that true goodness flies
  Above the plaudits of this earth.

The dreadful victory of the field
  'Twixt soul and self is never known;
Nor know we of the man who kneeled,
  In secret prayer, to God alone.

This struggle and this faith were thine;
  By man no victor's crown was given;
But even now a light may shine
  Around thy brows in highest heaven.

XXIV.

At times the patience of my soul
  With sudden rage is overflown;
I sparkle like an angry coal
  At which a furious breath is blown.

In wrath my frenzied numbers roar,
  A brandished sword in every verse;
And thus upon my foes I pour
  The flames of my prophetic curse.

May you, who so for money yearn,
  From thirst for gold be ne'er exempt;
And may each several coin you earn,
  Earn for you a distinct contempt!

May every virtue you can claim
  Be traded off, be priced and sold,
And made an offering of shame
  Before your loathsome idol, gold!

The miser's lust, the miser's fear,
  Possess you, soul and heart and mind,
Make you suspect love's holiest tear,
  And shut your door against your kind!

May money be your all in all,
  Your only gain, your only power,
The god on which your terrors call
  For comfort in your dying hour!

And, at that hour, may money dole
  Such comfort as it has in store;
As on your lonely beds you roll,
  May your hands clutch abroad for more!

So dying, in your coffins rot!—
  The plough pass o'er your nameless graves!—
Your gold be as the heavy shot
  That sinks the sailor in the waves!

XXV.

WITH passion yet my nature quakes;
  I quiver to the inmost soul,
Like an alarming bell that shakes
  After its tongue has ceased to toll.

After the bell has ceased to beat,
  What follows on the deafening din?
Good Christian people calmly meet,
  And solemn services begin.

So I, by stormy passion riven,
  Restrain my rage, devoutly bow,
And turn my asking face to heaven,
  But find a darkness on God's brow.

I know I strode a step too far;
  I reached with my audacious hand,
Above the privilege of my star,
  And caught at God's avenging brand.

I drop my head and pardon ask:
  This mandate sternly comes from Thee:
"O Poet, do thy human task,
  And leave the end of things to Me!"

XXVI.

I KNOW the men of after-time
With this fierce record will be vexed;
The comments on my culprits' crime
Will far outweigh the author's text.

I know howe'er that, now and then,
Some light will fall on what is said;
Some name be branded with the pen,
Some trespass find its proper head.

Their catalogue, with date and name
And due descent, shall surely last;
As how their race from nothing came,
And into worse than nothing passed.

Dead, damned, forgotten, save for me,
This rubbish, that I choose to save,
Shall surge into eternity,
The scum and outcast of the wave.

For them the foot of Time shall stand,
  His scythe hang idly, and his glass
Refuse to turn its blinding sand;—
  They shall not hide beneath the grass.

The men, themselves, to me are naught;
  Their crime, not them, is what I hate;
For as these fatal lines are wrought,
  I rather sorrow at their fate.

If my poor word were future law,
  I fain would give their names relief,—
Make them mere men of rags and straw,
  Mere scarecrows to their brother thief.

But men will delve in olden dates;
  I know the weight of what I do;
And how the scourges of the Fates
  Will drive the rogues in open view.

My verdict shall not be reversed:
  To me and mine no ruth they show:
They do their worst, I do my worst;
  But mine will be a lasting blow.

XXVII.

To-day should be a golden one:
  Within my calendar it stands
As that whereon love's chains were run
  Around my outstretched willing hands.

O dearest, on your candid brow
  I lay my kisses, but you start:
You see a cloud upon me now,
  You know a trouble in my heart.

Not thus our mated days began:
  That morn my kisses warmly fell;
For shouting Joy before us ran,
  And laughed, and shook his merry bell.

From end to end the world was bright,
  The heavens with glory overflown;
And when the stars came out at night,
  Their size and light had strangely grown.

I drew a picture of our days,
  What care might come, what mirth beguile;
A life that led through studious ways,
  Yet brightened by the Muses' smile.

We two have kept my picture true,
  And daily more and more it shone,
Till other fingers laid a hue
  Upon it, and it sank in tone.

Still hail with me our bridal morn,
  And spread the feast, and bring the wine:
Against this year of days forlorn
  It makes a little circle shine.

XXVIII.

Of old Amilcar called his son
  Before the gods, and made him swear,
While swords could strike or blood could run,
  Unending hate towards Rome to bear.

So thou, my son, with lifted hand,
  As solemnly avow to me,
Against this sacrilegious band,
  Perpetual strife and enmity.

My latter days small joy impart:
  Death comes in sadness, not in fear;
I feel his touch upon my heart,
  I hear his footstep in my ear.

Half-way I'll step my guest to greet,
  I'll face the shadow at my gate,
With, Welcome, friend! at last we meet:
  Receive my hand: thou hast tarried late!

But if I leave my work undone,
  My scroll of vengeance scant and strait,
To thy young hand, my only son,
  The fearful task I dedicate.

By night or day, through foul or fair,
  Pursue this purpose to its end:
God grant the sacred gift I bear,
  Thrice magnified, on thee descend!

Scourge wrong and fraud, scourge fool and knave,
  Nor care what tears or blood you draw;
Train your young sinews till you have
  The panther's tread, the lion's paw!

Tell liars that they lie; and tell
  The high-set scoundrel that his pelf
Was minted in the fires of hell,
  And there shall perish with himself!

Remember, that the holiest name,
  Earth knows, was merciless to wrong:
He reddened once with righteous shame,
  And in the Temple used the thong.

Men's lips shall follow thee with groans;
  Perhaps thou'lt win a martyr's crown;
But shout, like Stephen, blind with stones,
  Like Peter, hanging visage down!

The boldly good are martyrs yet:
  Who dares to scorn this sinful world,
Shall find his cross is ready set,
  And stones are gathered to be hurled.

Christ's mantle will not stretch and flow,
  Its scanty freedom binds and irks,
Man wears it in the church for show,
  But strips it off to do his works.

Be thou a Christian more sincere,
  Be just and true, be wise and bold;
Nor shame thy Master for a sneer,
  Nor sell Him for a bag of gold!

Be thou a soldier of the Lord,
  Armed with the sword, the cross, the lyre;
Press onward through the pagan horde,
  Nor fear, nor pause, nor turn, nor tire!

True poets are true prophets, sent
  To scatter fear through wicked lands;—
Take thy commission by descent,
  With prayer, and laying on of hands!

XXIX.

LET him who in my footsteps treads
  Be patient till the march is o'er,
Nor ask why 'round these brainless heads
  I swing the hammer of old Thor.

It is the stigma of our land
  That money is our only aim,
That all things bow to its command,
  That wealth is rank, respect, and fame:

That where our native face is seen
  This shameful passion shows its trace,
And hungry avarice makes keen
  The sharpened features of our race:

That art is dead, religion dull,
  Law idle, social virtue worse;
The sharper and the sharper's gull
  Breed and divide a common curse.

Some truth is wrapped in many lies:
  I hold it base the golden fool
Can win a reverence from our eyes,
  And bear so absolute a rule.

Nowhere, between the frozen poles,
  Is gold so reckoned in the count;
Nowhere the car of Mammon rolls
  So crushing and so paramount.

I grant, the rogue who bears a brand,
  Sometimes, may feel its fiery smart;
But yet the wealth in his command
  Is flattered, as a thing apart.

It soothes the pangs of his disgrace;
  It gives him power, if not respect:
With shouts we yield the rich man place,
  But whisper of the rogue's defect.

The purse-proud scoundrels whom I strip,
  Are bare that all may see them pass;
And when I wield my scornful whip,
  Through them I castigate the class.

Perhaps, like Canute on the shore,
I bid the raging waves subside,
Half-conscious that the next fell roar
Will bury me beneath the tide.

Come what may come, the word is said;
For man's behoof my best I give:
The martyr's ring may fit my head,
I perish, but the word shall live.

XXX.

The poet's word that stings and lives,
  Whose blow a subtile bane distils,
And breeds within the wound it gives
  The larva of a thousand ills,

To horny-hided brutes like these
  May be small matter for distress:
But if my ballads cross the seas,
  And thread the pathless wilderness,

And climb the linkéd mountains o'er,
  And down the sinuous rivers steer,
And warble at the poor man's door,
  And thunder at the rich man's ear;—

If every breeze of heaven that blows
  Shall blow these leaves about the land,
And every tide that ebbs and flows
  Shall wash them on another strand;—

If years shall give these graven lines
  A deeper meaning, and more strength,
And men discuss them o'er their wines,
  And women talk of them at length;—

Till, in all ears, each noteless name
  Is blared, as with a trumpet's blast,
I think, these knaves may feel some shame,
  Through all their brazen mail, at last.

XXXI.

If all the liars under heaven
  Could in one conclave congregate,—
To every tongue were charter given
  To hiss at thee its baneful hate;—

Were reason baffled by the din,
  And truth made blind, and justice dumb,
Till every shape and shade of sin
  Were piled upon thy guiltless tomb;—

Should men, deluded by the cry,
  Become thy enemies from choice,
Believe and circulate the lie,
  Defended by the general voice;—

Till none, heroically run mad,
  Dared lift a secret breath with me;—
For man, the thing would make me sad;
  It would not shake my faith in thee.

XXXII.

I KNOW not to what hearts I speak;
Perchance, to common, human ones;
Or humble hearts, hearts very meek,
Through which the general current runs.

Of him, the lowest of them all,
I ask in tones to suit his ear,
In bated breath, with dying fall
Made tremulous by ghastly fear;—

I ask, I say, this timid heart,
If your beloved were cold in death,
And o'er his sacred bier the mart
Should blow its sacrilegious breath;—

Each greasy huckster, dropping trade,
Should near the speechless body crowd,
And, by its silence venturous made,
Should spurn the dead man in his shroud;—

And brawl, and lie, and call him foul,
  And spit their rancorous bane about,
Until your faint and stricken soul
  Revolted at the general shout;

And, stunned with horror, you recoiled,
  In mute amazement, shocked to see
The man, you held most pure, so soiled
  With their abhorrent blasphemy;—

O feeble soul, would you retire?
  Would you, submissive, cringe and bow?
I answer, flaming into ire,
  You'd smite the miscreants on the brow!

XXXIII.

Faint not, strong heart, beneath thy grief!
  God hears thy ever-rising prayer;
Be not impatient for relief,
  If He unmoved thy wrongs can bear!

God sees the wicked delve and sow,
  He sees their thistle's purple crown
Flaunt in His suffering grain; but, lo!
  Ere harvest it is stricken down.

They build their Babel in His sight,
  From founding unto coping stone,—
Their pride is monstrous;—in a night
  They lie beneath it, overthrown.

His fires consume their cities proud,
  His floods rush through their palace-gates;
His prophet's voice sounds, clear and loud,
  Midst revelling princes and estates.

Nor can the humbler sinner shun
  The blow that snaps the crown of gold;
The liar, ere his lie be done,
  Before the crowd falls still and cold.

For where the fire bursts out at night,
  Men ask not is it hut or tower;
They only see a dreadful light,
  And shudder at a boundless power.

Therefore I will not deem this band
  Of knaves too mean to move God's wrath:
The lightning, slumbering in His hand,
  Is poised on its appointed path.

XXXIV.

Coarse miscreant, with the cringing back,
And shuffling feet, and flickering eyes,
And cloven lip whose hideous crack
Buzzes with swarms of countless lies!—

Sly reptile, with a faint, low tone,
Something between a hiss and whine,
Where spite and meanness meet in one,
Serpent and spaniel both combine!—

You have questioned, with your double tongue,
A dead man's fame; with brutal glee,
Hints and suspicions foul have flung:
Now, living culprit, answer me!

Know you not one whose tuneful voice
Redeemed your own ignoble part,
Whose songs shall make the land rejoice
When you are colder than your heart?

Puffed with your wealth, from street to street,
  In sordid dreams, you smiling sped,
Through ways where he, with shoeless feet
  In tatters, almost begged his bread,

Till, stung with want, disease, and shame,
  He gave the fruitless struggle up,
And drowned the buddings of his fame
  Within the drunkard's dizzy cup.

Nay, lower yet; from deep to deep
  His desperate spirit sank away,
Till, mad, men saw him laugh and weep
  Beneath the public light of day.

Did you stretch out your kindred hand,
  To help that starved and wretched soul,
Betwixt his shame and weakness stand,
  To save him from the certain goal?

No! in the pauper's filthy cell
  A stranger lodged the vagrant wretch,—
A poor, mad beggar! Is it well?
  How sleeps your conscience on this stretch?

I charge you, in the name of God,
  Go o'er your history day by day,
Since children sporting on the sod,
  With infant love at infant play,

He held you in his tender arms;
  Then touch that dreadful day of doom,
With all its horrors and alarms,
  That scowls upon him from the tomb.

How has your duty been performed—
  Your simple duty, nothing more—
Towards him whose baby life was warmed
  From the same father's scanty store?

I cannot say how deeds like yours
  Appear in other eyes, nor know
How even your fellow-rogue endures
  To look upon a thing so low:

But in the awful sight of God,
  There burns upon your brow a stain
That cries forever, "blood for blood!"
  Answer! where is your brother, Cain?

XXXV.

I TWINE to-day a victor's crown,
  To deck your champion's manly head,
And shade the terrors of his frown,
  O doughty foemen of the dead!

And since his deeds are new and strange,
  No common chaplet shall he wear;
Some fresh device I would arrange,
  That gest and guerdon may compare.

The curséd cross some leaves shall yield,
  And some the bough that Judas bent,
And some I'll gather from the field
  Where Joseph's brothers pitched their tent.

The viper of the proverb old,
  That stung the warming breast, shall clasp
The wreath together, fold in fold
  With him that bit against the rasp.

And strangling both, the wily snake,
  By which our common mother fell,
Upon his lifted crest shall shake
  Just Aristides' pearly shell.

The tears that banished Marius shed
  O'er ruined Carthage, shall be seen,
Like dew-drops, over all dispread,
  To keep the garland bright and green.

Wherever truth has been abused,
  Or man's ingratitude has lent
Its stain to aught, it shall be used,
  To add another ornament.

And when the work is wholly done,
  I'll plume the chaplet with this pen;
And having crowned your champion,
  I'll set him in the sight of men.

XXXVI.

OUR dead to us are never dead
  Until their memories are erased;
For oftentimes my hands are led
  To do the very things he praised.

Not in remembrance are they done,
  But timidly, as though he stood
Alive beneath the blessed sun,
  And smiled in his approving mood.

I sing some ballad gay and droll,
  Some quip he loved, ere going hence,
And think it strange he does not roll
  His laughter out, and drown the sense.

I do not think he cannot smile;
  I drop my head, and bend my ear,
And only ask myself the while,
  Is he so far he cannot hear?

It costs an effort of the mind,
A stretch of memory strong and dread,
Ere, groping through my brain, I find
The vision of his dying bed.

Through all this woful history,
I have called on him, by doubt oppressed,
And that he would not answer me,
Has moved me more than all the rest.

'Twere best to take this truth, unmixed
With any fancy: 'neath the sod
His rigid lips in death are fixed,
And silent as the lips of God.

XXXVII.

THE fierce, rebellious fall of rain
  Seems endless through this dreary night:
It pierces in my blind; the pane
  Is starred and streaked with watery light.

I know the grass upon thy tomb
  Is streaming, like a swimmer's hair,
And all thy roses' fragrant bloom
  Is floating on the boisterous air.

Thy reeking violets tangled swim,
  O'erburdened bows thy eglantine,
And stains of yellow soil bedim
  The lustre of thy myrtle vine.

The treacherous damp hath slowly slid
  Through oozy roots and melting clay,
To spread upon thy coffin-lid,
  And help corruption to its prey.

f

Alas! alas! I can but sigh;
  Yet on my care it seems a stain,
That thou so desolate shouldst lie;
  And tears are falling with the rain.

XXXVIII.

WITH song of birds, and hum of bees,
  And odorous breath of swinging flowers,
With fluttering herbs and swaying trees,
  Begin the early morning hours.

The warm tide of the southern air
  Swims round, with gentle rise and fall,
And, burning through a golden glare,
  The sun looks broadly over all.

So fair and fresh the landscape stands,
  So vital, so beyond decay,
It looks as though God's shaping hands
  Had just been raised and drawn away.

The holy baptism of the rain
  Yet lingers, like a special grace;
For I can see an aureole plain
  About the world's transfigured face.

The moments come in dreamy bliss,
  In dreamy bliss they pause and pass:
It seems not hard, on days like this,
  Dear Lord, to lie beneath the grass!

XXXIX.

If I could value at its height
  The power I have, or take the praise,
I daily hear, on faith, some might
  Would animate these failing lays.

Some token of the master-hand,
  Some notes struck out with confidence,
Some fiat from the throne, would stand
  As offset to my impotence.

The feeble heart of self-born doubt
  Ill aids a purpose great and strong;
A grand truth, timidly set out,
  Oft drifts upon the side of wrong.

Sometimes I quake with voiceless rage,
  Or dull the sense of holy love;
And, like the novice on the stage,
  Half fear to see my audience move.

No trust within myself I feel;
  I sing my songs, I know not why;
The maid who sings beside her wheel
  Is silenced by a stranger's eye.

But she whose tingling ears have heard
  The "*brava!*" and the plaudits loud
Of rapturous men, is only stirred
  To utterance by a listening crowd.

I never heard these plaudits ring:
  I cannot take the poet's place,
And boldly to the nations sing,
  Without a blush upon my face.

In my own weak and faulty way,
  I pray you, let my song proceed;
For, somehow, God and nature say,
  These rhymes were purposed and decreed.

To one God gives the robin's tone,
  To one the carol of the lark,
To one the mocking-bird's, to one
  The owlet's, drearier than the dark.

Taunt not the owlet with his shrieks,
  Nor say he lacks the others' skill:
A voice of nature through him speaks,
  According to God's plan and will.

XL.

AGAINST the words which current pass,
Whose wisdom even folly owns,
That he who keeps a house of glass
Should be the last at throwing stones;—

The fool who first attacked my dead,
Forgot his race's history,
Forgot the crystal o'er his head,
That show-case of their infamy.

I marvel, ere, in search of sin,
About the town he chose to roam,
His virtuous quest did not begin,
Like prudent Charity, at home.

There, marked and ready for his eyes,
Is guilt no eloquence can gloze,
Which all men see, and none denies,
That stinks beneath the public nose;—

That rots and festers in the light,
  To draw mankind's abhorrent stare;
That, in the very depths of night,
  Glows with a foul putrescent glare.

Ere he set forth to scour the land,
  And cleanse the dunghills of the earth,
He should have used his sweetening hand
  About the mansion of his birth.

Surely this modern Hercules,
  In sallying, must have stumbled o'er
The loathsome heap that taints the breeze,
  The common nuisance at his door.

Is virtue, like philosophy,
  A showy saint, of mere parade,
Who flaunts an outside purity,
  Yet lives at home an arrant jade?

If he at whom this shaft is flown
  Dare ask what name is here arraigned,
He is the only man in town
  Who needs to have the thing explained.

XLI.

A SCULPTURED stone to-day was laid,
  A sacred cross, above his breast;
And as the masons wrought, I prayed
  The heart beneath might lie at rest.

For, turn it as I will, a doubt,
  That grieves the spirit, haunts my head,
Lest, haply, this indecent rout
  Disturbs the slumber of my dead.

For I would have no harsher noise
  Than grasses rustling in the breeze,
Or little birds that sing their joys
  Amongst the many-nested trees;

Or the slow river's lulling sound,
  Or the low piping of the wind,
To breathe a drowsy song around
  The couch whereon he lies reclined.

A sound that through the senses steals,
  And partly breaks their quiet deep,
Till a half consciousness reveals
  The very blessedness of sleep.

And nature, more than kind to me,
  Has calmed her voice to my desire;
She gently sighs through herb and tree,
  And sinks the pitch-note of her choir.

And I, myself, who, in the hush
  Of serious evening, grieve and moan
Beside his grave, without a blush,
  Have felt my manhood drop its tone.

All things assuage my troubles sore,
  And strive to make my sorrow light;—
Only these fierce hyenas roar
  Above him in the coward night.

XLII.

If sorrow is love's fruit, and love
  A tinted blossom of the morn,
That drops ere noontide from above,
  A wreck for man's maturer scorn;

If man should leave the flower for maids
  To twine amongst their wanton hair,
And bear the bitter fruit to shades
  Of lonely philosophic care;

If icy wisdom is life's prize,
  And love an artificial want,
I fear the frozen brains, thus wise,
  Are in their wisdom ignorant.

From point to point they slowly climb,
  And time outruns their tardy pace;
But Love, that mocks the foot of Time,
  Bears revelation in his face.

A revelation somewhat dashed
  With clouds of doubt, but partly riven,
As though God suddenly had flashed
  His presence on us out of heaven.

Yet filled with yearnings vague and vast,
  That beckon from the top of things,
With longings for some glory past,
  With consciousness of growing wings;

With sense of something overhead,
  That glimmers through this dusty strife,
And shines victorious on the dead,
  Above the darkened vale of life.

Towards that the spirit pants to move,
  On that Faith turns her patient eyes;
And this aspiring heat of love
  Strikes blind the wisdom of the wise.

It is an awful truth revealed,
  Which only Love can bear to see,—
God's dateless charter, signed and sealed,
  That warrants immortality.

XLIII.

THE dreary morning of my woe
  Has slowly crept to light again:
Cold winter day, arrayed in snow,
  And stripped of flowers and waving grain!

The land is dumb and stiff and grim,
  And wrinkled o'er with frosty rifts;
Through heaven the hurrying vapors skim,
  On earth the hissing snow-storm drifts.

The naked branches of the wood
  Are shivering in the ashen light;
A seal is laid upon the flood;
  The evergreens are piled with white.

No cattle browse, no small bird sings,
  No motion breaks the dismal sleep,
Save where yon roaring torrent flings
  Its icy burdens down the steep.

Love knows no season: forth I go,
  Upon my holy mission bent,
And on thy grave the fair white snow
  Seems nature's cloth of sacrament.

I kneel, and with me kneels the dead;
  The bread is broken, the wine is poured;
We eat and drink with Him who bled
  To join our souls, with Christ our Lord.

XLIV.

If mere existence be Love's scope,
  And earth his brief and petty scene,
I cry, from scorn of cheated hope,
  'Twere better Love had never been!

Why should man toil, by slow degrees,
  To fit his soul for things divine,
While Pan is peering through the trees,
  And Bacchus pours his reeling wine?

Hope, born of Love, in grief replies,
  "Why draw in trouble with thy breath?
When Adam woke in Paradise,
  What knew he of predestined death?

"He ate and knew, he sinned and fell,
  He saw his blood upon the sod:
Death's woful tale were yet to tell,
  Had he been faithful to his God.

"When love arose within thy soul,
  My cheering whisper said to thee,
'Stars wax and wane, but this shall roll
  Its orbit round eternity.'

"Why doubt and fear? Take love on trust,
  Nor charge thy title with a flaw;
No special grace requires thy dust
  Beyond the universal law.

"The promises I made were clear,
  They cannot pass, they keep their worth.
You say, 'Fulfilment draws not near:'
  They shall not be fulfilled on earth.

"You stand beneath the darkened porch,
  And quarrel with the builder's plan;
Anon, I'll rise, and light a torch,
  And show the true abode of man.

"What thing on changing earth can stand?
  What work of human hands shall last?
You draw a picture on the sand,
  Then shriek at every wave and blast.

"Love dwells within the heart of heaven;
Creating light, he light preserves;
Such glimpses as to man are given
Are more than faithless man deserves.

"Despair not, though Fear cries, dismayed,
'Death throws a shadow far and wide.'
Whatever casts on earth a shade,
Looks brighter on its heavenward side.

"Though to thy senses Death may be
A grisly phantom of the night,
We call him, in eternity,
An angel of transcendent light.

"No higher instinct of the soul
Bears fruit on earth; it blossoms there;
It strives to burst from time's control;
It seeks an outlet everywhere.

"These aspirations are not vain;
The callow eaglet beats his wing;
The nestling lark begins the strain
That he in highest heaven shall sing.

"So far from Death defeating Love,
  Death saves him from this earthly strife,
Till through his native realm he move,
  The spirit's strength, the spirit's life.

"Be true to Love, and Love for thee
  Shall bear at last his perfect fruit:
As well doubt immortality
  As doubt its highest attribute."

XLV.

These wild, unquiet thoughts that rove
From land to land, yet find no rest,
That brood amongst the clouds above,
Or skim the billow's foaming crest;

That wander with the vagrant bee,
Rolling in joy from flower to flower,
Or, eagle-like, stand silently
On crags that front the sunset-hour;

That enter in the ghastly tomb,
And grope amongst the clammy dead,
Or take the soul's enfranchised plume,
And circle towards its fountain-head;

That struggle through the greedy crowd,
With hand of guilt and heart of steel,
Or, with repentant anguish bowed,
Fall prone where sinners only kneel:

Whence come these thoughts? Are they inborn?
  Am I possessed by heaven or hell?
Am I more fit for praise or scorn?
  I wonder much; I cannot tell.

XLVI.

Blow gently, southern breezes, blow
  Around the circle of this tomb!
Blow down the locust's hanging snow,
  And blow the roses into bloom!

Come from thy golden realm of day,
  With spices fresh upon thy lips,
And breathe across the new-mown hay
  And thyme that with the dew-drop drips!

Glide softly, rippling river, glide,
  And hither all thy music send!
Through beds of sedge and lilies slide,
  And slender reeds that rise and bend!

Commingle with thy mellow voice
  The springs that gurgle from the ground,
And make thy cataract rejoice
  In the full splendor of his bound!

Lay kindly, gorgeous sunset, lay
  Upon this tomb thy rarest dyes,
And with the showery vapors play,
  And arch thy rainbow in the skies!

And ere thy fiery race be run,
  And thou in sombre clouds must fall,
Gather thy sinking rays in one,
  And flash a glory over all!

Sing lower, moody poet, sing,
  Or let thy song in silence die;
Thy sorrow is a jarring string
  In nature's grander harmony!

In reverential worship crave
  Forgiveness for a vain despair!
God listens now; and this lone grave
  Is, as an altar, set for prayer!

XLVII.

Standing upon this grave, I view
  The world with my anointed eyes.
They pass along, a motley crew,
  The people, with their works and cries.

Through many a mazy path they run,—
  They join, they cross, they part, they meet;
But all their ways converge to one,
  That ends beneath my very feet.

The weariest struggler here shall rest,
  The fiercest cry here gasp for breath;
The bondman with his lord may jest
  In this old commonwealth of death.

So high my dizzy stand is fixed,
  I cannot judge men's deeds aright;
They seem in vain confusion mixed,
  Mere motion, indistinct to sight.

For if yon emmet hoards or spends,
  Or this one means to buy or sell,
Or what that other's act intends,
  Is more than I can truly tell.

Or if that be a sad parade
  Of mourners following the dead,
Or warriors, armed with spear and blade.—
  Yon pygmies winding down a thread.

But this I know: a million strands,
  Converging to this central place,
Some spider wove, and all the bands
  Climb here, with pallor in the face.

Each by his separate thread ascends,
  As partial fortune may allot;
But each, with empty hands, here ends,
  And in his season is forgot.

XLVIII.

BEFORE the scornful face of death,
  How small and purposeless appear
The works that cost us panting breath,
  And caught the world's applauding cheer!

The man I loved toiled out his day,
  His plans he laid, his aims he won;
He saw, before he passed away,
  His fruitage rounding in the sun.

What though his enemies despise
  The ended story of his cares?
I doubt not his seraphic eyes
  Now scorn the labor more than theirs.

To the freed intellect, whose stand
  And outlook is eternity,
These twinkling worlds are grains of sand
  That tumble in an airy sea:

The finite senses' highest flight,
  Mere aspiration after good,—
A blind man reaching for the light
  He feels, but never understood.

And he, perchance, stands side by side,
  And smiles upon the deeds he did,
With him who, in a kindred pride,
  Built the sky-cleaving pyramid.

For what are earthly ills and joys,
  Before the soul's eternal gaze,
If not remembered as the toys
  She played with in her childish days?

What aim of man is high or low,
  What perishes, or what survives,
In the great shock and overflow
  That levels all our temporal lives?

We worms spin less or greater cells,
  We fashion webs in which to die;
What are the reptile's empty shells
  Unto the air-borne butterfly?

A purpose runs throughout the plan;
I doubt it not; though I but see,
In what we call the life of man,
The gambols of his infancy;

A childish effort to achieve,
A mocking play with straw and sand,
Which all the frightened children leave,
Forgot in sleep, at death's command.

For if we dwell in peace or strife,
Or found a throne, or sing a lay,
Is little in the coming life,
So we but worship and obey.

XLIX.

I, FOR my part, would rather tear
  The trophies from Achilles' head,
And suffer in the wrath I dare,
  Than raise my arm against the dead.

The dead are God's; His awful hands
  Rest on them; waving swords arise
Above them, like the fiery brands
  Before the gates of Paradise.

'Tis hard to brave God's wakened wrath;
  It never sleeps, it never tires;
It hangs above its victim's path,
  It bursts beneath his feet in fires.

Behold it in the lightning's glow,
  And hear it in the thunder's roar,
And in the hungry waves that sow
  With helpless wrecks the crumbling shore!

10

It walks with pestilence by night,
 It shapes the chances of the day,
And when the sky is fair and bright,
 It darts from heaven a withering ray.

It guides the reinless avalanche,
 It bursts the river's ancient bound,
And makes the boldest visage blanch
 With shudders of the yawning ground.

It lies in ambush everywhere,
 It joins with folly in the dance,
Mirth's freshest wreath its temples bear,
 It wakes the light of beauty's glance.

Its age no sum of years can tell;
 It tracks the soul beyond the clay,
It lights the lurid fires of hell,—
 It sings forever in this lay!

L.

WHAT special baseness of our kind
  Can seize upon the scheming head,
That turns its vile, irreverent mind
  To conflict with the harmless dead?

The monster who will raise his hand
  To strike a child or woman low,
Sears on his front the coward's brand;—
  What 's he who strikes the dead a blow?

I have sounded all the foulest things
  Within the foulest human hearts,
Yet nowhere can I find the springs
  From which so base a motive starts.

The seven deadly sins I shook,
  Until their damned adherents wailed,
Yet found no face that did not look
  Upon the grave with eyelids veiled.

Even common Avarice I wrung:
  He spoke not; miserably he smiled,
And from his burdened bosom flung
  A loathéd and degenerate child.

I knew the horror not by name;
  My hair arose, my blood ran cold;
He called it, with a blush of shame,
  His bastard son, "mere Lust of Gold."

I traced it on from spot to spot,
  I marked its way by slimy streams,
Till, like Eve's toad, I saw it squat
  At my rogues' ears, to shape their dreams.

LI.

THE beef-faced brute who leads this band,
  And serves as mouth-piece for the crew,
I pity; for I understand
  His school-days were but brief and few.

I'll take him as I find him then,
  Rude, coarse, ill-mannered, vulgar, blunt;
Expecting nothing from the pen
  But the swine's voice, a simple grunt.

Grace and indulgence shall be his:
  He cannot speak without abuse
Of something, though that something is,
  Chiefly, the language which we use.

LII.

To-day I faced my enemies;
In smooth-tongued converse, veiling hate,
We talked with hypocritic ease,
And brought our business in debate.

And all the time, the knave, who stung
The heart that warmed him, snake-like stirred;
And all the time, their leader's tongue
Slaughtered the English word by word.

And round about me winked and leered
The common herd; and, one and all,
Piled lie on lie until I feared
The Lord, perforce, might hear them bawl.—

Until, in wonder and alarm,
I gazed on traitor, rogue and clown,
Expecting God's avenging arm,
Each moment, would come flashing down;

And they, who bartered in the street
His priceless truth for treacherous gold,
Would fall death-stricken at my feet,
As Ananias fell of old.

One fool, lob-sided and bare-browed,
Mindless of home, in spiteful glee,
Of gibbeting my name talked loud,
As though he shared the hangman's fee.

One blustered, swaggered, stamped, and swore,
Till conscience was by rage beguiled;
And one, whose hair was silvered o'er,
Babbled, unnoticed, like a child.

But all the while the subtler cur,
Whose bark had harried on the pack,
Was out of sight: such things prefer
To stab one's honor in the back.

So each, according to his kind,
Wriggled, and licked his cloven tongue,
And lied, as fancy led his mind,
And round about his venom flung;

And I, amidst this reptile throng,—
  Giants in fraud, but dwarfs in wit,—
Stood calmly, and composed a song,
  Like Ragner in the serpents' pit.

LIII.

I CANNOT pass that threshold o'er
  Without a sinking of the soul;
A spectre haunts the open door,
  And round the walls low murmurs roll.

A voice seems calling from within,
  That should not speak on earth again;
The voice sounds ghostly faint and thin,
  But, O my soul! how strangely plain!

It cries for vengeance at my hand,
  It dooms me to this task forlorn,
It drives me on as with a brand,
  It sneers my weakness into scorn.

The hopeless fate of ancient Greece,
  That ground resistance into dust,
Ladens that mandate, and I cease
  To struggle, and am onward thrust.

I do my part. The place is cursed
  Beyond man's prayers; the curse must fall;
A desecrated grave has burst,
  And poured its darkness over all.

LIV.

WHY sorrow for the hopeless past,
  Or strive again to re-create
That shattered mould, in which were cast
  The hardened features of our fate?

I know not; but my soul rebels
  Against the tyranny of time,
Fights inch by inch, and dearly sells
  The freedom of her native clime.

Chained, scourged, oppressed and overthrown,
  Defiance fires her quenchless breath;
She spurns the conqueror on his throne,
  And dares him to the test of death.

She will not yield the past as gone;
  She stretches back her yearning eyes;
She counts her memories one by one,
  And calls them all realities.

Beyond the gulfs of death expand
  Great visions, and she forward springs;
Yet will not loose her clinging hand
  From its fast hold on earthly things.

Time cowers before her dauntless tread;
  She sweeps into eternity,
With her immortal wings outspread,
  Trailing her whole grand history.

LV.

If to the soul, as to the sense,
  The past were cancelled, and no more,
And this divine intelligence
  To mortal weakness rendered o'er;

So that the soul, for countless years,
  Must stand amid the heavenly host,
And see, through her despairing tears,
  The past irrevocably lost;

I would bear my immortality
  With something like contempt, and lift
A prayer to death to set me free
  From such a poor, imperfect gift.

To find eternity unfold
  A shattered and disjointed ring,
In which time lords it as of old,
  Were to the soul a sorry thing.

Our aspirations were undone,
  Our hopes an overshot mistake,
If past and future, merged in one,
  Be not the life to which we wake.

LVI.

Eternal God, before Thy face
  How nature and Thy creature, man,
Shrink their proportions! time and space
  Contract, and narrow to a span!

What is man's life within Thy sight?—
  The moment that we climbers stand
Toppling upon a dizzy height,
  With yawning death on every hand.

We vaunt the knowledge gained by sense,
  We bound creation with our pride,
Forgetting, in our ignorance,
  That what reflects must also hide.

Our mirror shows a glorious sight:
  A re-created world we find
Within ourselves; its forms delight;
  We ask not what may be behind.

And man, the vain, presuming fool,
  Who measures all by time and space,
Picks up his little ell-wand rule,
  And gravely marks a planet's place.

And yet why will the soul assail,
  With anxious, stubborn questionings,
The secret of this polished veil,
  And beat it with her fiery wings?

Until the glass, in which we see
  The world so fair, be ground to dust,
The greater sight and mystery
  Is hidden, and received on trust.

O Lord, break down this blinding bar,
  And let my struggling spirit pass
Beyond the orbit of the star
  Just glimmering through the optic glass!

I pine for knowledge unperceived,
  I doubt the evidence of sense;
I trust the truth will be achieved
  When, in the soul, I journey hence!

LVII.

One counsels me to drop my scourge,
  To live at peace, and strive to please:
Not for the rogues' sakes would he urge
  His plea, but for my private ease.

If with myself my duty stopped,
  And the commission of my God
Were cancelled, long ere this I had dropped
  To nothing in my kindred clod.

The first faint stir of human pain
  Had left with me no after-smart,
Could I have rent my aching brain,
  Or probed with steel my sorrowing heart.

I scorn the soul that never felt
  A blow to shake its stolid ease:
Itself it knows not. Death, soon dealt,
  Were more than life on terms like these.

LVIII.

If good and evil are but one,
  Or to one end and issue made,
And that effulgent central sun,
  That makes the brightness, casts the shade;

If our deluded moral sight,
  The brightness seals, the darkness blinds,
And all the lines 'twixt wrong and right
  Are vain confusions of our minds;

If we who hurry Sin aside,
  And set him on a throne abhorred,
Make, in our intellectual pride,
  A power almost above the Lord;

If what Omnipotence permits,
  He forms and sanctions and sustains,
And smiles to see our stretching wits
  Defining that which He ordains;

If this faith-strangling creed be true,
  Through all its tangled subtilties,
We have but followed out the clue
  Where lead our new philosophies.

Rather for me the brimstone bed,
  The satyr devil of the child,
Or those rude horrors that o'erspread
  Men's fancies when our creed was wild.

Sin is God's sorrow; and the soul
  That never feels the inward strife,
As hell and heaven together roll,
  Has never lived the spirit's life.

Give me, O God, the agony,
  The war with evil, up and down!
Give me Thy tearful sympathy,
  The triumph, and the shining crown!

LIX.

Long golden days and mellow nights
  Have lit and dimmed this earthly scene,
The trees have bloomed in reds and whites,
  And now again are tawny green,

Since, in the glooming winter snow,
  I laid thee from the world apart,
And felt the chilly season flow
  Inward upon my shrinking heart.

Long summer-days may come and go,
  In sunshine or in silver rain,
The scented flowers may bud and blow,
  The fields may sprout in fruitful grain;

Yet in the fiercest blaze of day,
  When all the panting world stands still,
One thought will wrap the whole in gray,
  And strike me with that wintry chill.

LX.

Is grief a weakness of the mind,
  A useless, discontented strain
Against the galling links that bind
  Our lives in fate's remorseless chain?

Does God, with hard, averted ear,
  Refuse to hear His children cry?
Does every sob and sliding tear
  Draw down the brow upon His eye?

If this be so, in vain you say,
  He in His image fashioned me,
And breathed within my sentient clay
  His fervent immortality.

I reason back from man to God,
  With God's own warrant for my creed,
And delving in the dusty clod,
  I find at last the primal seed;

And cry, that every throb of pain,
  The present and the after-smart,
Is echoed o'er and o'er again
  In God's vast, semi-human heart.

I keep this faith, to hearten dread,
  That every tear of king or churl,
In pure and honest sorrow shed,
  Shines in God's crown a lucid pearl.

LXI.

My cries of wrath are fitful cries;
  As an attack of sharper pain
That, in a lingering illness, tries
  The frame, then passes off again,

Is this possession of my hate,
  That intermits but still returns;
Now drives me flaming towards my fate,
  Now smoulders, but, though smouldering, burns.

And, sometimes, while my fancies play
  Amongst the vapors of my fire,
I cast my knotted scourge away,
  And rest the culprits from my ire.

I only rest: anon my lash
  Shall fall more sternly than before,
And measured melody shall dash
  Its waves into a savage roar.

LXII.

I SAT with men; few words were said;
  Of pregnant things we mused and talked,
When he, who had betrayed the dead,
  In through the doorway shambling walked.

He stooped beneath his load of sin,
  The Atlas of a world of lies;
His wrinkled and cadaverous skin
  Hung trembling o'er his toad-like eyes.

The chase of gold had worn him lank,
  And dried his blood, and pinched his face;
Our common manhood downward shrank
  Within him, at its own disgrace.

This wretch who dared not speak the truth,
  With God to back him, seemed so vile,
That anger softened into ruth,
  And tried to give a sickly smile.

I almost stretched a helping hand,
  To raise him amongst men again;
But started, for I saw his brand,—
  The long-forgotten brand of Cain!

LXIII.

WHAT cuts thee from thy fellow-wretch,
And, in the press of busy day,
Makes gaps of solitude to stretch
About thee in the peopled way?

I never saw thee, arm in arm,
Companioned by a brother knave,
Planning some scheme of fraud or harm,
Such as thy coward heart might brave.

Men talk, with an averted face,
Of gold to thee, and there they end;
There is no outcast to abase
Himself by calling thee his friend.

Cold serpent, never on thy head
Had woman's eye one glance to fling;
She shrank, with an instinctive dread,
That saved her from thy treacherous sting.

Art thou self-conscious that for thee
  No kindred heart shall ever swell,
That to thy meanness there shall be
  Companionship,—no, not in hell?

LXIV.

I WATCHED at eve beside thy tomb,
  With something like a pang of shame;
For snails had crawled from out the gloom,
  And dragged their tracks across thy name.

Across thy sacred name I saw
  The foul defacers' oozing slime;
And marvelled at the higher law
  That made such sacrilege no crime.

The worms were fled, the tomb defiled;
  In vain my wrath; I could but weep.
Then knelt I down, and, as a child,
  I faintly prayed myself to sleep.

Dawn broke at length; I raised my head;
  The desecrating stains had flown;
And on the tablet of the dead
  Some hand had laid a lily down.

LXV.

Arch traitor, in thy restless bed,
  I wonder oft if thou dost see
The warning phantom of the dead
  Appear, and hover over thee.

If in the hush of middle night,
  He comes, a shape of ghastly fear,
And blasts thy vain-averted sight,
  And whispers in thy tingling ear.

Beneath his touch how creeps thy skin,
  How stirs to life thy matted hair,
How chilly and how deadly thin
  Thy blood crawls backward to its lair!

What says he then? Does he arraign
  Thy baseness and thy lust for gold;
Or stab thee, o'er and o'er again,
  With kindness, as he did of old?

Doubtless, thou hast thy own defence,
  Some self-deluding lie to tell,
Some poor excuse, to recompense
  The tortures of thy inward hell.

Can that avail, when sleep has stripped
  The conscience of deceiving flesh,
And memory has open ripped
  Her wounds, that ache and bleed afresh?

I cannot say. I see thee lie
  Beneath his gaze; around thee yawn
Great gulfs of darkness; and a cry
  Goes struggling upward for the dawn.

LXVI.

If all this passion run to waste,
  And leave no seed upon the land,
And scornful men pass by in haste
  The painful culture of my hand;

And like some monstrous natural thing,
  That leaves no kindred progeny,
The wild, disordered songs I sing
  Lapse into mere nonentity;—

'Twere vain and false denial then,
  To laugh, and innocently say,
More harm is in the piping wren
  Than in my ballads' whole array.

My bitter song is not unheard;
  The thoughtful angels listening sit;
I tremble on from word to word;
  For shall I not be judged by it?

LXVII.

I DO not draw for man alone
  This magic web of woven air;
I think one soul, that hence is flown,
  Is wistful how his loved ones fare.

I fear that all my tears and sighs
  Disturb his clear immortal day;
So I abase my running eyes,
  And sigh as softly as I may.

And since I know he loathes a wrong,
  Whene'er I touch my scornful strings,
I mean that he shall hear my song,
  And peal it till the welkin rings.

Yet not to pierce his heavenly ear
  With the cruel edge of human woe,
I deck it out in minstrel's gear,
  And move to music sad and low.

I little care what brow is bent
  Against my purpose. Men may fill
The land with sneers at my intent,
  So he impute to me no ill.

The laugh, the jeer, the look of scorn,
  Are naught to me; they pass me by,
As the light fleecy cloud that is borne
  A moment through an April sky.

A moment, and the frown is fled,
  The mouth is dumb, the scoffer gone;
While through the world a song has sped,
  And in immortal youth lives on.

LXVIII.

If I were well assured of this,
  That what I write shall never die,
I would fold my hands in dreamy bliss,
  And down to death would calmly lie.

For I am haunted by a doubt
  That some unworthiness of mine,
Or of my song, may blot me out,
  And raze my record line by line.

Not the pure heart, the pure design,
  The mind's high sanction, nor the might
Of conscious power that, strong as wine,
  Befools my judgment as I write;

Nor all the loud and frothing stuff
  Of windy rhetoric, wrung to rhyme,
Have in their substance salt enough
  To save a verse from gnawing time.

Beyond all this, above it all,
  Some subtile essence, undefined,
Keeps fresh the songs that rise and fall
  In surges through the common mind.

I can but lay on God that fear;
  And trust that, in some low degree,
Far in the poets' shining rear,
  The after-times may think of me.

LXIX.

DEAR Lord, to Thee I cry aloud!
  My task is greater than my strength;
My spirit fails, my knees are bowed,
  I sink beneath my load at length!

Thus far I struggled, and thus far
  Mere human courage bore me on:
I followed forth a setting star;
  The guide is lost, the star is gone!

O feet that toiled up Calvary,
  O brow that bore the bloody crown,
O mortal God, I call on Thee,
  Bruised by the world and trampled down!

I, clinging to Thy cross, invoke
  Thy pity on a sinner's prayer!
Grant me a respite from this yoke—
  Destruction, rather than despair!

My race is run if here I fail,
  And all my panting labor vain ;—
Tear Thy pierced fingers from the nail,
  And touch me into life again !

LXX.

I, WANDERING by this bitter shore
  Of death and sorrow, sometimes turn
My vision inward, and explore
  Myself, the more myself to learn.

What shock of chance has rent this breach
  'Twixt nature and my ranging eyes,
And made her visions dumb to teach,
  And hushed her starry harmonies?

Where has the silver lily birth?
  Where winks the early violet?
In what fair corner of the earth
  Shines morn on meadows dewy-wet?

Where do the linkéd seasons run
  Their mystic dance through cold and heat?
Where flash the swallows in the sun?
  Where sing the robins, full and sweet?

What stills the cataract's shout of strength;
  The chorus of the chanting waves,
That hurl their Titan bulks at length
  On beaches and through sounding caves?

Where is the pageant of the night,
  The burnished shield of dauntless Mars,
Soft Venus with her liquid light,
  And all the congregated stars?

Where is the sense that, through the whole,
  Caught glimpses of the inner truth,
And whispered somewhat to my soul?—
  Where is the glory of my youth?

Dead nature haunts me like a ghost,—
  A hollow shell of broken laws;
But this appalls my spirit most,—
  I cannot be the man I was.

LXXI.

What man shall set his hardened brow
Against the cause that I maintain?
Or, looking in God's face, avow
He holds my motives in disdain?

Above myself I strive to move,
Earth tempts not my determined flight;
The holy frenzy of my love
Aspires to touch the central light.

What power of earth shall turn aside
A zealot from his single aim?
What human courage shall abide
The will that no reverse can tame?

The meanest thing that crawls the sod
May be the link on which depends
The grandest providence of God,
And wonderfully work out its ends.

I give my body to the dust;
  I wing my spirit to the sky;
I blindly grasp the hand I trust,
  And follow, never asking why.

God's purpose is above my mind:
  O'er dubious ways I hold it fast;
And trust He mercifully will find
  Some refuge for my soul at last.

LXXII.

Through the dark path, o'er which I tread,
  One voice is ever at my ear,
One muffled form deserts the dead,
  And haunts my presence far and near.

In times of doubt, he whispers trust;
  In danger, drops a warning word;
And when I waver from the just,
  His low, complaining sigh is heard.

He follows me, with patient tread,
  From daybreak until evening's close;
He bends beside me, head by head,
  To scent the violet or the rose.

And sharing thus my smallest deed,
  When all the works of day are past,
And sleep becomes a blessed need,
  He lies against my heart at last.

Dear ghost, I feel no dread of thee;
 A gracious comrade thou art grown;
Be near me, cheer, bend over me,
 When the long sleep is settling down!

LXXIII.

I FOUGHT with spectres in the night;—
 I, sinful, feeble, faltering, lone,
With all hell's legions in my sight,
 Strove on, with cry, and sob, and groan.

Vague, shapeless things, of fear and doubt,
 Assailed my soul; with sudden start,
Temptations stretched their fingers out,
 And almost touched me on the heart.

Alive with evil nature seemed;
 She spawned and hatched my myriad foes;
Hell from the lily's centre gleamed,
 And fumed its vapors from the rose.

Earth's surface crawled with loathsome life;
 The streams ran blood; the very grass
Grew into snakes, and endless strife
 Writhed through the foul, abounding mass.

The rocks and trees took features on,
  And stared dumb horrors in my face;
Like sheeted ghosts the clouds were drawn,
  Great, mournful shapes, in endless chase.

And through the whole, a wretched tone,
  That killed the spirit in my breast,
Ran on forever,—a low moan
  That never, never hoped for rest.

It sighed o'er life, it sighed o'er death,
  It found no comfort anywhere,
Save in the self-afflicting breath
  Of its own desolate despair.

I found a voice: I shrieked aloud
  To him I love, my dearest dead:
Dawn smote the farthest eastern cloud
  With a low streak of dusky red.

He glimmered from a rising star;
  His face was pitiful and mild.
Dawn grew; the phantoms fled afar;
  He looked upon my face, and smiled.

LXXIV.

WERE beauty nearer the divine
  Than beauty is, its power were vain
To move this steadfast heart of mine
  Beyond the line of faint disdain.

Who wins my heart, must find the way
  A purer love has grandly trod,—
Must track it towards the fount of day,
  Sheer upward to the feet of God.

O loving heart, serenely bold,
  The way is plain, but hard to tread;
It lies through regions, vast and cold,
  Between the living and the dead!

Come hither, at the twilight hour,
  Beneath this pine-tree's solemn gloom!
Pluck, as a spell, a grave-side flower,
  And I shall greet thee from the tomb!

LXXV.

A SERVICE done to me is naught;
The gauds and trinkets of this world
I hold as more than dearly bought
When my contemptuous lip has curled.

The purest fame that man achieves
He wins himself, against our bent;
The grudgéd homage he receives
Is but hard-wrung acknowledgment.

The name that stands through envious time,
Stands unsupported by the race—
In man's despite—a power sublime
That holds in awe the abject base.

What were our Shakespeare's deathless fame,
Dependent on man's jealous praise?
He moves before us, with God's claim
To kinghood flashing from his bays.

True greatness reigns by right divine,
  Within itself it keeps its state;
With all the votive wreaths we twine,
  Ourselves we do but elevate.

Praise is cold service. More than fame
  I prize the gift of human love;
And humbly tearful, at its name,
  Towards my race I trembling move.

O fount of joy! O well of tears!
  I throw myself upon thy brink,—
I, thirsty, famished, weak with fears,
  Reel to thy singing waves, and drink!

LXXVI.

Ye men of evil, ye who dare
  Assail the consecrated grave,
And lay its awful mysteries bare,
  What impious issue do you crave?

Is this last fane, whose walls are hushed
  Against fierce Mammon's godless jar,
This sanctuary, to be crushed,
  At length, beneath his golden car?

Are ye not satisfied to see
  The wrecks of sanctity around,—
Man's faith, man's love, life's poetry,
  Laid prostrate with the common ground?

Shall this sole refuge of a race
  That groans in bondage, self-imposed,
Be made a public market-place,
  Where hucksters' stuffs shall be exposed?

Beware! you pull a temple down
  Whose shelter may one day be dear,
Whose silence you may pray to drown
  The curses howling in your ear.

Before whose desecrated door
  You will crawl, with anguish and dismay,
And pray God's mercy to restore
  The broken arch, and smooth the way;

That you, yourselves, may enter in;
  Less fearful of the hell to come,
Than of the unrelenting din
  That drove you downward to the tomb.

What if it be no refuge then?—
  If your misdeed be paid in kind?—
And round your graves, forever, men
  Shall blow a storm of slanderous wind?

LXXVII.

In hazy gold the hill-side sleeps,
  The distance fades within the mist,
A cloud of lucid vapor creeps
  Along the lake's pale amethyst.

The sun is but a blur of light,
  The sky in ashy gray is lost;
But all the forest-trees are bright,
  Brushed by the pinions of the frost.

I hear the clamor of the crow,
  The wild-ducks' far, discordant cry,
As swiftly out of sight they go,
  In wedges driving through the sky.

I know the sunshine of this hour,
  Warm as the glow of early May,
Will never wake the dying flower,
  Nor breathe a spirit through decay.

The scarlet leaves are doomed to fall,
  The lake shall stiffen at a breath,
The crow shall ring his dreary call
  Above December's waste of death.

And so, thou bird of southern flight,
  My soul is yearning for thy wings;
I dread the thoughts that come to light
  In gazing on the death of things.

Fain would I spread an airy plume
  For lands where endless summers reign,
And lose myself in tropic bloom,
  And never think of death again.

LXXVIII.

Now thou art gone, in vain to me
  Is any stir of human praise;
Such trophies as I won for thee,
  Lie in the shadow of my days.

I see, with melancholy scorn,
  My bay-wreath falling, leaf by leaf;
It lies in ashes, soiled and torn,
  O'er-stained with tears of rage and grief.

My lyre is hushed: the breezes wake
  Its trembling strings to better cheer;
My listless fingers only make
  A murmur in death's moody ear.

Partly because some spirit strong
  Urged me to sing, I sang awhile;
But more than half my faulty song
  Was raised to draw thy partial smile.

Think as I will, I cannot bring
  My mind to deem thee far, nor strange
This voice to thee; and so I sing,—
  Only I sing to suit thy change.

To thee it matters naught, to me
  But little, what my ballads' fate:
They shall receive a smile from thee,
  Hereafter, in some happier state.

LXXIX.

Great God, I cannot bear this thing!
  Shall his, the name I honored so,
Hang out for every wasp to sting,
  And every carrion-fly to blow?

I held thee sacred here on earth;
  Thy precept was my guiding light;
How holy, how divine thy worth
  Shines on me from its starry height!

Dear Soul, within thy mortal clay
  Was nothing selfish, nothing small;
Shalt thou become the helpless prey
  Of the foul worms that o'er thee crawl?

Thy name was carved in spotless white;
  So shone the record on thy death;
Shall skulking cowards of the night
  Defile it with their slanderous breath?

Forbid it, God! Thus humbly bowed,
I cry for justice at Thy hand!
Flash downward from a stooping cloud,
And raze the liars from the land!

LXXX.

My soul is open to thy eye,
  Thou seest me simply as I am;
No sin can hide, or shuffle by
  Thy piercing vision clear and calm.

I know 'tis hard for mortal clay
  To bear, unawed, a light divine;
Nor dare I confidently lay
  Before thee this frail heart of mine.

The vileness I, myself, perceive,
  Must magnify beneath the view
That sees hell's total broadness cleave
  A gap between the false and true.

In trembling I pursue my ways;
  But surely I may trust that He,
Who so enlarged thy mortal gaze,
  Enlarged thy mortal charity.

LXXXI.

If this sole solace of my grief,
  This power to shape a dreary lay,
Were silenced, and the blest relief
  Of thought in music reft away;

I would have burst in rhetoric bold,
  Such as shook Macedonia's king,
Or poured the words, from lips of gold,
  At which false Catiline took wing;

Or traced again, with fiery pen,
  The scorn that made Salmasius rave
Before the mockery of men,
  And jeered him to his wretched grave.

For, lacking utterance to my woe,
  I must have writhed as one possessed,
And tossed my wild arms to and fro,
  And rent my hair, and beat my breast.

Therefore thank God that in mild song
  He still permits my pain to shroud;
And when I thunder o'er the throng,
  'Tis only from a golden cloud!

LXXXII.

Not pity, but a deeper sense
  Of something graver, stirs to birth,
At every sight of grief intense
  That moves this melancholy earth.

The vulgarest and meanest show
  Of sorrow is a sacred thing,
That fills the chambers of my woe
  With flutterings of an angel's wing.

I smile no more at pain absurd:
  A holy presence treads the ground
Where'er its sobbing voice is heard,
  And I,—I tremble at the sound.

No soul takes flight, but wings the way
  On which my own Beloved has flown:
I kneel, and with the mourners pray:
  I see all sorrow through my own.

LXXXIII.

Perhaps I make my grief too plain;
  Perhaps the sharpness of its smart
Strikes too directly on the brain,
  And fails to reach the deeper heart.

Some things are clearer, barely caught
  In shadowy outlines, that suggest
A feeling rather than a thought,
  Quick fancy filling up the rest.

If I have erred through stress of truth,
  And made my picture's tones too high,
Know that this vision of my youth
  Cut a clear line against the sky;

And every light and shade I saw
  Was terribly distinct to me:
I am too dull to err by law;
  I can but paint the thing I see.

LXXXIV.

WHAT evidence lies round about
The soul in its eternal jars
With Doubt? For, sometimes, prying Doubt
Would thrust his fingers in the scars;

Count every nail-hole, touch the wound
Made in the body; ere he heed
The words of witnesses around,—
"This is the very Lord indeed!"

Facts keep our mounting faith in awe:
Linked by stern sciences they sit,
And rather lean upon the law
Than on the hand that fashioned it.

Small comfort comes from gathered weeds,
Or sums of years, or cloven stones,
Or all the dry material creeds
That gather round the mammoth's bones.

The Soul, not blindly, but with eyes
  That search through darkness for the day,
Looks round the circle of the skies
  From the dim windows of the clay.

She sees a strange, uncertain light,—
  Perhaps the dawn of day to come;
She questions Science, on her height,
  But the proud Sibyl's mouth is dumb.

She can but loose her offspring, Doubt,
  Upon the Soul, to mend her cause,
And haunt the spirit in and out,
  And prate of matter and its laws.

Let Science, and her sceptic child,
  Walk humbly amongst earthly things;
For all heaven's whiteness is defiled
  When beaten with her dusty wings.

Give Science all that she perceives,
  Nor let her pride by that be blown;
For what the dullest soul believes
  Is more of worth than all that is known.

LXXXV.

The hopes, on which our spirits live,
Are now completed truths to thee;
Thy soul no longer can misgive
The shaping of the last decree.

The end of prophecy is thine,
The law that lies in seeming chance,
And all the tangled schemes we twine
Are simple to thy single glance.

The banded stars beneath thee spin;
They cannot hide their secret power;
Thou know'st the mystery within
The blooming of the earliest flower.

From sphere to sphere thy soul ascends,
Earth fades beneath her cleaving wings,
Till, gathering all creation's ends,
She broods above the crown of things.

Poised in thy grand eternity,
  I question thee, majestic Soul;
Has earth no more regard from thee
  Than as an atom of the whole?

Or like a man who, days and nights,
  Has travelled, and at length is come
Above his city's myriad lights,
  And only sees the light of home,

Art thou, thus gazing from afar?—
  And when thy clear perceptions part
The mingled systems from one star,
  Comes there a tumult in thy heart?

LXXXVI.

I MEET thee, sometimes, in the deep
Of midnight, on that neutral ground,
'Twixt life and death, which men call sleep:
We meet, and part, without a sound.

God will not grant that, even in dreams,
Thy voice shall gladden me again;
So thy familiar presence seems
Unreal, a phantom of my pain.

I cannot lose the heavy thought
That thou'st another life begun;
I feel our lives can ne'er be brought
Again to mingle into one.

So something strange invests thy mien,
Dear Mockery; and I seem to grow,
Myself, a phantom in the scene,—
A silent portion of the show.

I speak not, for my words were vain:
  I see, upon thy changeless face,
That no reply would come again;
  I touch the limit of the grace.

Oh! grace unlimited! 'Twere vile,
  If even my hungry heart asked more
Than the warm sunshine of the smile
  That falls upon me as of yore.

I know that look of love and trust,—
  That musing look of tender pride;
'Tis more than when it lit thy dust;
  'Tis now sublimed, beatified.

Yet a vague fear perplexes me:
  Beneath that smile, sincere and bland,
Something upon thy face I see,—
  Something I cannot understand.

LXXXVII.

WHEN my dead roses bloom once more,
  And these dark daisy-leaves with stars
Of white are powdered o'er and o'er,
  And through yon rusty lattice-bars

The jessamine thrusts its yellow tips,
  And the bright pansy pranks its head,
And the tall lily's pallid lips
  Part slowly, and from green to red

The beaded grapes begin to turn,
  And round the outskirts of the lawn
The woodbine blossoms faintly burn,—
  Ah! then, perhaps, on me may dawn

The morning of a better day;
  And this sad heart its woful hue
May reverently put away,
  And deck itself in something new.

LXXXVIII.

WHEN I am turned to mouldering dust,
  And all my ways are lost in night,
When through me crocuses have thrust
  Their pointed blades, to find the light;

And caught by plant and grass and grain,
  My elements are made a part
Of nature, and, through sun and rain,
  Swings in a flower my wayward heart;

Some curious mind may haply ask,
  "Who penned this scrap of olden song?
Paint us the man whose woful task
  Frowns in the public eye so long."

I answer, truly as I can;
  I hewed the wood, the water drew;
I toiled along, a common man,—
  A man, in all things, like to you.

LXXXIX.

THEY tell me thou art far away,
  That all my cries to thee are vain,
That I but rave above thy clay;
  Thou canst not hear my voice complain;

That heaven, in mercy to the dead,
  This cloudy cope o'er earth hath thrown;
Else were the blesséd spirits fed
  On sorrows keener than our own.

It may be so. I cast about
  For faith; but never find its seeds
In men who dole God's mercies out
  According to their narrow creeds.

No man e'er saw a spirit's wing
  Outspread before his mortal eyes;
But is man's sense the only thing
  On which his wiser soul relies?

Love's vision is a sense divine:
  I trust its truth, when I avow
That, standing face to face with mine,
  A spirit fronts my spirit now.

XC.

I STOOD amidst an angry throng,
To plead, to question and to hear;
Some scowled with predetermined wrong,
Some lowered with greed, some paled with fear.

My purpose grew before their eyes;
Scorn filled me, as with potent wine;
I felt the dead man's spirit rise,
And stir a stronger life in mine.

Then one who bore our common shape,
One who must some time fill a tomb,
Sprang up, and tore hell's gates agape,
And poured on earth its boding gloom.

With flaming face, in words uncouth,
A thousand frenzied things he said;
Blasphemed the simple grace of truth,
Outraged the living and the dead.

About me, in the listening crowd,
  I saw full many smiling stand,
Whose servile necks erewhile had bowed
  With favors at the dead man's hand.

They dared not speak upon his part,
  Nor make truth's sacred cause their own;
Only one brave and loyal heart,
  Who loved him for himself alone,

Arose, and boldly faced the storm,
  And said the thing which he thought right:
And as he spoke, methought, his form
  Grew radiant with supernal light;

And heaven's great portal open swung,
  And all the angels softly stole
A little out, to hear his tongue
  Thus pleading for their fellow-soul:

And ever since, this man of men
  Has walked before me glory-crowned;
A virtue flows into me when
  I touch his raiment from the ground.

XCI.

I TRUST in man. Not all are base;
  Not all are pricked by grasping self,
To show the hollow double face
  That masks the shameful love of pelf.

Fierce eyes have shone, bold tongues have hurled
  Defiance at my sordid foes;
And here and there, about the world,
  A tear has dropped upon my woes.

And chiefly thou, so wholly pure
  In thought, in act, in spotless fame,
Stern scorner of the golden lure,
  Whose soul is whiter than thy name;—

I grasp thee with a brother's hands;
  I hold thee as the dearest prize,
Bequeathed to me by him who stands
  No more before our sorrowing eyes.

And thou, dear friend of later date,
  Whose wisdom guides the subtle pen
That oft has shaped the nation's fate,
  And dealt out destiny to men.—

Strong in thy calm self-sacrifice,
  That questions not the doubtful end,
Nor counts the marketable price
  Of service to a trusted friend.

You two are strangers. Pray you, be
  By no mere custom kept apart:
My love holds high festivity;
  I join your hands within my heart.

XCII.

WHERE violets and daisies spring,
  And buttercups nod to and fro,
And the young grasses' golden ring
  Clasps the pine's mossy trunk below;

Where the wild locust's branches drop
  Their scented snow in eddying showers,
And the magnolia's leafless top
  Stars mid-day with its silver flowers;

Where ivy climbs, and myrtle creeps,
  And the small lily's bells are hung,
And the proud laurel darkly keeps
  Its wreaths for glories yet unsung;

Where the broad river slowly lags
  Round grassy points, or softly draws
Its currents through the tangled flags,
  Chased by the breeze's fitful flaws;

Where the wood-robin rears her brood,
  And, at the dewy ends of day,
Pours, by no fear of man subdued,
  The tender music of her lay;—

There lies a grave; and thither fly
  My wildest thoughts, and there they cease;
And all I ask has one reply:
  That grave but whispers, "Peace, peace, peace!"

XCIII.

I PITY him who holds his grief
No higher than a passing sigh;
And casts about, to find relief,
With nature's tear-drops in his eye.

Who seeks the world to drown his care,
Who leads the laughter of the gay,
And lays his sacred sorrow bare,
For any breath to blow away.

Who dulls his heart, and drugs his brain;
Is pleased, and strives in turn to please;
That he may blunt the edge of pain,
And live again in selfish ease.

The grief that rent my breast has shown
The wonder of my heart to me;
And, mirrored clearly in my own,
The great heart of humanity.

Supremest wonder of the whole!
  O heart divine! whose narrow space
Reflects before the gazing soul
  Heaven's vastness, and God's vaster grace!

XCIV.

In robes of woe, before me stood
 A silent figure. Towards the ground,
His features, muffled in his hood,
 Were bowed with sorrow most profound.

I questioned him; but no reply
 Was mine, save what might be expressed
By the long quaver of a sigh,
 Or hands that beat his troubled breast.

I loosed his robe, with meaning kind,
 I drew the garment from its place;
His splendor struck my senses blind;
 An angel shone before my face!

His smile said more than many words:
 He tarried not; he gazed on high;
His pinions flashed, like brandished swords,
 And clove amain the cloudless sky.

I followed him with longing view;
  He did not vanish from my sight;
His form diffused itself, and grew
  To be a portion of the light.

XCV.

THE day arose in dismal black,
  In dismal black crept out the morn;
Noon passed unheeded; and the rack
  Grew darker, thicker, more forlorn,

As down, behind yon wooded ledge,
  The unseen sun supinely rolled;
Nor did he tinge the lowest edge
  Of evening with his fiery gold.

Deep and more deep the darkness grew,
  As the weird midnight hour drew nigh;
Until, from out the west, there flew
  A little breeze, and swept the sky.

And all the stars together shone;
  And, here and there, a planet glowed;
And the moon's waned and broken zone
  Made silver of a ragged cloud.

Then praised I Him who dimmed the day,
  And made the evening's glory dull,
Only to wipe the stain away,
  And make the night more beautiful.

XCVI.

CAN time, that makes the memory
A fading record, faint and pale,
So gain the mastery over me
That what is written here shall fail?

And like a vain and faithless girl,
Who reads the letters of her youth,
My brow shall knit, my lip shall curl
O'er that which once was meant for truth?

And other love, and other grief,
New scenes, new faces, and new deeds,
Shall pour a balsam of relief
In every wound that aches and bleeds?

It may be that a calmer day—
God grant it!—may be given to me;
But where the steel has rent its way,
There, too, the lasting scar will be.

XCVII.

Let me not scorn my better self,
  And drag my nobler nature down
To that degrading scale of pelf
  That measures out the red-faced clown,

Who, in his coarse, indecent way,
  Would chaffer for a good man's fame;
And give his stock of lies in pay,
  And shut for gold his mouth of shame.

Bought peace, at any price, is dear;
  Peace, with such knaves, can only stand
When it has wrung from beaten fear
  Its title with the naked brand.

I sound a challenge to my foes;
  I plunge into the doubtful fight;
To right and left I deal my blows:
  I ask no aid, no greater might

Than that which falls from God above;
  Or from the Soul who silent stands,
Gazing on me with patient love,
  Stretching o'er me his blessing hands.

XCVIII.

It seems that even rogues like these
  Can find worse rogues to be their tools,—
Fellows who lie for paltry fees,
  Shufflers of precedents and rules.

Men who would take a cause from hell,
  And nostril-deep through foulness wade,
Serving the Devil quite as well
  As God, if they were duly paid.

With any trade I quarrel not:
  Corruption strikes the tree in bloom;
And some must clear away the rot,—
  Mere scavengers by nature's doom.

Well, let them go! One, only one,
  At this eternal bar shall stand,
Who fawned before me in the sun,
  And in the darkness tore my hand.

Within thy wretched memory
  I cause the spectral past to tread;
Each step is marked by grace to thee,
  Accorded by the kindly dead.

Was it for thee, of all men born,
  To turn, before the grass had sprung
Upon his grave, and blend thy scorn
  In chorus with each lying tongue?

Is this a benefactor's due?
  Does scorn become a thing like thee,
Bred 'twixt the pot-house and the stew,
  To each its worst deformity?

I marvel at thy ingrate heart,
  Thy falsehood and thy purblind sense;
But palsied falls my rhyming art
  Before thy bare-browed impudence!

XCIX.

O MAN of serviceable mind,
  Whose memory can only strain
Back to the things wherein you find
  A present hope of selfish gain!—

How luminous, how crammed with acts,
  Are all your recollections then!
How glibly slide the lying facts
  From rattling tongue and flowing pen!

But where your history seems to frown,
  And shake a finger at your purse,
How soon your eloquence is blown,
  And stricken with a silent curse!

Strange but convenient intellect!
  That follows but the golden track;
I'll test its merit and defect;
  I'll question it upon the rack.

Do you forget the youth whose look
  Was humbled before fortune's ill,
Who bent above a musty book,
  And drove with sighs a hireling quill?

Do you forget who, pace by pace,
  Advanced him onward to his good,
Against their wills who knew him base,
  Until a man with men he stood?

Who nursed his fortune till it grew;
  Whose counsel added gain to gain;
Ever beside him, strong and true,
  With hand and heart and planning brain?

The man who raised you from the dirt,
  By the mere greatness of his mind,
Failed but in this, and felt the hurt,—
  He made you not what he designed.

He meant to make you something more
  Than nature willed,—wise, true and bold;—
The vileness of your soul ran o'er,
  And spoiled his purpose in the mould.

So Heaven, in primal Adam's birth,
  Miscarried. The created still
Spurns the creator; and your earth
  Was not exempt from mortal ill.

It is not strange that you forget;
  You are most mortal; and to ask
For gratitude or vain regret,
  Were to assume God's future task.

Or have you with those memories,
  So aptly lost, forgotten, too,
The Dead who sleeps but to arise,
  And hold a reckoning with you?

C.

The primrose in the valley blooms,
The snowdrop swings its silent bells,
The willow droops its tangled plumes,
The maple's tufted blossom swells;

Long sweeps of tender grass ascend
The hill-side, towards the melting snows,
And where the climbing patches end,
Full-flowered, the low arbutus blows.

A duller sense than mine should feel
The stir in nature's warming soul;
It makes the shouting bluebirds reel,
And bursts the violet's twisted scroll

O sullen darkness of the heart!
O fruitless torpor of the brain!
When will your clouds and frosts depart?—
When shall I come to life again?

CI.

THE yearly miracle of Spring,
  Of budding tree and blooming flower,
Which nature's feathered laureates sing
  In my cold ear, from hour to hour,

Spreads all its wonders round my feet;
  And every wakeful sense is fed
On thoughts that, o'er and o'er, repeat,
  "The Resurrection of the Dead!"

If these half vital things have force
  To break the spell which Winter weaves,
To wake, and clothe the wrinkled corse
  In the full life of shining leaves;—

Shall I sit down in vague despair,
  And marvel if the nobler soul,
We laid in earth, shall ever dare
  To wake to life, and backward roll

The sealing stone, and, striding out,
  Claim its eternity, and head
Creation once again, and shout,
  "The Resurrection of the Dead"?

CII.

We poets hang upon the wheel
  Of Time's advancement; do our most
To hide his inroads, and reveal
  The splendors which the world has lost.

Ruins with ivy-leaves we twine,
  We flower the path of crippled Use,
And, sometimes, hold as half divine
  What others count as old abuse.

We see regality in kings,
  And something like a sacred power
In sceptred hands and jewelled rings:
  We will not trust the present hour.

So Science and her sneering tribe
  A cry of fierce derision raise;
And ever have a taunt or gibe
  To fling against our harmless ways.

We but lament. We cannot lay
  A feather to impede their force;
Creation is become their prey;
  They claw and rend her soulless corse.

We but lament. We miss God's hand
  Upon our radiant mother's brow.
Tearful, and full of fear, we stand;
  Tearful, and full of fear, we bow.

Science and Avarice, arm in arm,
  Stride proudly through our abject time;
And in their footsteps, wrangling, swarm
  Their own begotten broods of crime.

We cannot flatter. Since our seed
  First flowered within the Chian isle,
No poet's song was raised to feed
  The famished passions of the vile.

Hopeless but endless war we urge
  Wherever guilt uplifts its face:—
Witness, in my right hand, this scourge,
  Red with the blood-drops of the base!

CIII.

GLORY to God! This blessèd hour,
The tender touches of the day,
Drew me, by some mysterious power,
A little from myself away.

Great Nature lay with open breast,
And palms outspread, beneath the sun,
And dreamed of all the flowers, that drest
Her olden summers, one by one.

Her dream possessed my drowsing brain,
Young Eden opened on my view;
I saw its sunshine and its rain
Pour lightly on the sinless Two.

They listened to the pastoral bleat;
The lion fawned before their tread;
With trusting eyes they set their feet
Upon the harmless serpent's head.

One spirit moved all earthly things;
Communion with the great and small,
The tree that grows, the bird that sings,
Was theirs; they understood them all.

How long I dreamed I cannot say:
Upon her poles the great earth wheeled,
And cast her mortal age away
In what her visioned youth revealed.

I woke to a discordant din,
A sting that almost took my breath:
The din was as the howl of sin,—
The sting was as the sting of death!

CIV.

I, SIGHING o'er the happy past,
  Yet murmur for the time to come;
And, like a shipwrecked voyager, cast
  On land, above the flying foam,

Look, from my shelter, o'er the sea,
  To catch the glimmer of a sail;
And think my solitude to be
  Worse than their lot who, in the gale,

Went down amidst the strangling wave;—
  Quick exit from the endless strife
That I reluctantly must brave,
  To keep my body's wretched life.

I stand upon a barren shoal:
  The life that was seems passing fair:
I stretch the vision of my soul,
  And fill the azure depths of air

With flashing crowns, and snowy wings,
  And saints, rejoicing as they meet,
And the seraphic choir that sings
  Forever at God's quiet feet.

CV.

IF any good may come to me
  From the cruel thorns o'er which I tread,—
Soft touches of humility,
  That bow to earth my chastened head;

I shall not thank the evil things,
  That served as Heaven's dumb instruments;
Nor give their many wholesome stings
  The merit due to good intents.

Out of the vileness of their hearts,
  They hissed and stung: God's mercy stood
Between us, and allayed the smarts,
  And from their evil wrought my good.

CVI.

I KNOW that I shall never cease,
 Dear Soul, to walk one path with thee;
Though on my head the years increase,
 Thy image lives in all I see.

Thou risest with the vernal bud,
 Thy footstep shakes the summer grain,
Thy lips with autumn's fruity blood
 Are wet, and through the wintry rain,

And rigid ice, and driving snow,
 Thy ghost stands solemnly apart,
With thoughtful eyes that sternly glow
 Their light upon my inmost heart.

I murmur not. I would not fly,
 Dear, dreadful vision of my brain,
Thy awful love and ruling eye
 To save one twinge of selfish pain.

It strengthens me, thus living half
  Within the brightness of thy soul,
To see the age's tear or laugh,
  Yet live supreme above the whole.

No change of fickle time can be,
  By which the race is saved or wrecked,
That I shall not desire to see
  Swept over by thy intellect;

And all its secrets clearly shown
  Before thy wide supernal eyes,
That I may catch some truth unknown,
  And grow, beneath thy wisdom, wise.

I hold my lot a higher one,
  If not a happier, than to stand
The blazing point in fortune's sun,
  The mortal idol of the land.

For though 'tis joyless, thus unfit,
  To bide so near heaven's open gate,
Such chance as mine had never lit
  The darkness of our earthly state,

Hadst thou not drawn me by thy love
  Half from this chrysalis of clay,
And taught my feeble wings to move,—
  Wings pinioned still, and scant of play.

Following thy will, I onward bear,
  Through aid above my strength or worth,
With wings that cleave the heavenly air,
  With feet that drag the common earth.

CVII.

WITH pious hands I close thy tomb,
  Whose dreadful lids have stood ajar,
As the great angel's book of doom,
  Throughout this long and weary war.

Sleep now in peace! Against the day
  Thy Janus'-gate no longer yawns;
Sleep, while the earth that bears thy clay
  Speeds onward through a myriad dawns!

Sleep, in the darkness so beloved
  By those who lie beyond our sight!
In decent slumber, and unmoved,
  Pass thou thy long, untroubled night!

While round thy grave the myrtle creeps,
  The pine-tree drones its dirge on high,
The blue-eyed violet yearly weeps,
  And o'er thee bends the placid sky.

And I, and she who loves me most,
  And those who proudly bear thy name,
Shall reverence thy sacred ghost,
  And stand as champions for thy fame.

The curs that bayed at thee are dumb;
  The liars strangled with their lies;
A thousand honest voices hum
  Thy praise, and not a foe replies.

No sound shall come to vex thy ear:
  Thy small domain of flowery sod
Is hallowed. Sleep, without a fear,
  And wake but at the voice of God!

THE END.

www.ingramcontent.com/pod-product-compliance
Lightning Source LLC
LaVergne TN
LVHW010742120826
845150LV00009B/1384